The Scribbles
of a
Broken Heart

Regina Ducey

After all the heartbreak, I thought my heart was surely done.

Adding up all of the seconds, minutes, hours, days, weeks, months, and years I've wasted feeling less than, feeling worried, unloved, worthless, sad, scared, and downright awful, has felt absolutely sickening. As I count the days I feel this overwhelming sadness. To have ever let another human being defile me in such a way, to voluntarily hand my heart and mind over to another to only have it be thrown around so carelessly with the intention of handing it back to me more broken then when it was received, to have allowed the opinions of others to dictate my life. Oh, it's been exhausting! I lived this way for far too long..

If I could gather all of the tears I've cried from these moments we would never fear another drought, we would have deeper oceans and rivers running wild for lifetimes, and I could put my favorite quote to use. "You can't stop the waves, but you can learn to surf." - by Jon Kabat-Zinn

It's not easy being hurt over and over by the people you thought loved and cared for you, the ones you selflessly gave your time and heart to. I lived this way for a long time because I was not aware of my own potential. I didn't see that this is not how I should be treated by them or by myself. It took many years for me to find my strength, to see my worth and to move on from the hurt that lived inside of me. It was no easy

3

task and it came at a price. One I was glad to pay, for I left with my freedom and my sanity.

I hope you, my reader, can find your light within yourself, the strength that is hidden beneath your worries, and the knowledge that you have gotten through 100 % of your bad days.

So join me as I scribble my way through my experiences around dishonestly, disrespect, abuse, mistreatment, addiction, codependency and more.

Disclaimer: This book is filled with events that can be triggering. Read with caution and if you feel overwhelmed by your emotions contact your Doctor, Therapist, or Local Hotline.

My Poetry

The beginning I do not start
but I dive right into the deep
the deepest parts of my heart
I'll tear these pages apart

My words here are formed
take them and see past them
I must take a moment to warn
deep feelings and thoughts
are pressed within the hem

An Irresponsible Heart

The realization sets in
love a distant feeling
My emotions feel like a sin
this fear has me reeling

My heart so irresponsible
it now only knows how to beat
I use to feel the impossible
now I feel so incomplete

I wonder if I will heal
if my passion will come back
Will I ever be able to deal
or will I be lost to cardiac

Letting Go of the Unhealthy Thoughts

The late hour has her restless
her mind just cannot stop
She left her life of madness
it was easy for her to drop
No more lies
from the man she loves
No more sorrow
from the loss
Said good-bye
to the push and shove
She let go
of her unhealthy thoughts

Picking up the Pen

After hours of crying
I realize
Damn
this heartache sure makes for some good poetry

Love Yourself First

You need to learn
to be with yourself
before you can ever
fully be with another

That goes the same
with Loving

Take All Of Me

the darkness
creeps up like a cold bitter night
a shiver down my spine creates
the heaviness of my chest becomes unreal
you've opened me up like a gate

my secrets lay out for you to see
my scars they all tell a story
all my demons disappear in this abstract moment
at this moment I don't have to worry

you take all of me
you feed my soul
we move so perfect together
there's so much to see
no way to let go
you assure me
all of this we can weather

this spark creates such an intense warmth
my breath
so crisp
so quick
our souls have become so entwined
I now have nothing left to give

Forward In Fear

He calls to me
every inch of my spidery veins catch fire
The echo of darkness fills my ears
a tone so deafening
"Come to me"
a spine-chilling statement
The reluctance in my feet keep me standing still
Do I even have a choice?
As the fear spreads throughout me
forward I march

Us...

I'm pulled to you like a magnetic power
my heart is a thorned rose
such a strong beautiful flower
Your mind
so intense
such an amazing wonder
Our love
a strike of lightning
as loud as thunder
Your eyes grow distant
I see their complexity
I search for you almost desperately
That intense divine world you find yourself in
take me with you let me be your yin
For you are my yang
we are opposite but one in the same
for you my love
you are my twin flame

Draining Flame

There's beauty in certain moments
moments you never want to change
I'll hold those moments closest
this love has began to feel so strange

A new feeling has come to surface
something's changing within
I must stand with courage
I believed you were the flame to my twin

My soul searching for you
my heart; how it has ached
Oh if you only knew
how much you made my inner quake

I will leave your deception behind
for you are quite the trickster
How had I become so blind
true love is now a distant whisper

A Belligerent Heartbreak

I open my eyes
holding the pain of yesterday
I cannot see
much of anything
Looking deep within
I fear there's nothing to say
Filled with guilt
brings such suffering

The sting sits in my soul
scratching at its deep crevice
The sting takes such a toll
darkness embedded

So how is the pain of today any different?
How is another loss so heartbreaking?
Over the years my heart has grown so
belligerent
but I cannot be so forsaking

My love flows deep within my veins
my passions so surpassing
What I feel for you will always remain
well past my final passing

The Confusion In Lust

Mistaking love with lust
we begin this new adventure together
When I awaken from the lure
I start to lose that feeling of pleasure
Who is this man?
I thought I was in love
Now I'm seeing his truth
and all he's made of
It sends a shiver down my spine
a darkness over my heart
How did I miss this?
It must have been there from the start

My Words hold Power

The passion bleeds from my fingertips
but never my mouth
With the words that I choose
things end up going south
Taking my words from the page
feels foreign to me
But these words know all
they tell what's been seen
Writing them down
then walking away
Keeps them in my mind
the place they forever stay
Never being able
to take my own advice
These words like no air to fire
they breathe no life

Heartbreak

A simple word
filled
with so much emotion

Getting Through

As I speak of my situation
I can feel their judgements
"How does someone so strong allow for this to
happen?"
It's such a simple complex answer
I am human
and sometimes I too
wonder if my creation was flawed
I feel as if I was built with too much feeling
to much emotion
Like no one else I've ever met
But
at the end of the day I know
I have gotten through 100% of the bad days
through 100% of the engulfing emotions I feel
Sometimes knowing that alone
Helps

R

E

S

P

E

C

T

I'll say it once more

Respect

This doesn't mean
Wiping the shit off your shoe's onto me
The doormat!
Smearing my name everywhere you go
The Bitch!
Stealing my time with lie after lie
The Fool!
Pushing me to the ground with all of your hate
Worthless!
If you can't Respect me
If you can't refrain from calling me these
meaningless bitter words
Then simply leave!
I know my worth
This is not it!

A Heart's Sad Moment

Your hands are like sandpaper
clenching onto my heart
The grips so tight
it's tearing me apart
The emptiness of a full room
suffers in silence
The silence echoes so loudly
that we can no longer hide it
The smallest tasks
have grown uncomfortable
It's hard to remember a time
when things were actually comfortable
Does my pain mirror yours
or are you insulted?
Have I come here alone?
Am I being compulsive?
The anger on your face
makes me want to flee
So I leave your side
giving you time to breathe
I'll sit alone
with all of my thoughts
All the while I'm hoping
this is something it's not
Then we'll wake up tomorrow
and you'll be fine
I can't forget
I need some more time
But by then we start this
all over again
And here I am

→

wishing that I never let
anyone in
You'll continue with your anger
hiding all other emotions
Never telling the truth
is how we became broken

"Never telling the truth
is how we became broken."

Silence

And there it is
Silence
Complete ear ringing
high pitched
deafening
Silence

Take it All Back

Please go. Take the invisible chains you've built around me off and take this bleeding knife from my heart. Pull the string of lies from within my ears and rip this mouthy tongue from behind these lips. The lips that once found comfort in yours, now tastes of deceit and anger. Take this aching soul and fill it back with what you have taken. Take the sore from these unused bones that hold this frail body up in bed alone with intense emotion. Just please go and let me be. Let me be who I was before I met you, before you tainted this fierce and enormous loving gentle heart.

The Mirror to your Sadness

I'm worthless
A Bitch
No Good
A Loser
The words that fall from your lips
create a perfect picture
Let your art flow
paint my body with your judgements
Fill my head with your fear
smelling of pungence
Your sadness shows on my skin
as you hide behind your mirror
On your face lay a grin
darkened by a broken shimmer
These words that you choose
to describe my faults
Only mirror the reflection
you've locked inside your very own vault

He Says

" I hate you! "
     " You're worthless! "
          " No one will ever love you! "
             " You're lazy! "
" I'm sorry "
     " I'll change "
          " I didn't mean it "
             " Don't go "

Table For Two

This table for two
has become so crowded
Unsaid words
filled with despair
Frustration has
us surrounded
Speaking gets
us nowhere
Your uncaring eyes
shoot right through me
I feel
your dark energy
The ending
I do foresee
Why do we sit
here so unhappy

Angry Love

His hits come easy
the coldness of his tone so cruel
Darkness keeps them busy
he uses it as his only tool
No words to be said
there's just nothing left to say
Is it all in her head
of course he'll have his way
Another wall built
they sit in silence
She's filled with so much guilt
as she suffers in compliance
While he's comfortable in his anger
she shivers in fear
He worships this growing cancer
he'll gladly watch as she disappears

Prisoner

A prisoner!
That's all that I am here
What I thought was my home
really a jail cell
Opening my mouth
no matter what I say
condemned
I can't
Breath
Eat
Sit
or Stand
A prisoner
That's all I am!

His Love

He looks at me like I'm his worst nightmare
the darkest of dreams filled with despair
Speaking to me like an enemy
his war has begun
he has no empathy
Bringing me down
with a sharpness of tongue
Looks of daggers
the scorch of the sun
Burning every inch
of my soul
He'll never stop
until I let go
His hatred so raw
it eats me alive
My self esteem now gone
it's taken a dive
I need to move on
I need to let go
His hatred will live on
no matter how much love to him I show

Feeling Psychologically Uncomfortable

Your filled with so much anger
Your face
swallowed in hatred
Your body
shaking in despair
Your mind
overgrown in vines of doom
And your heart
so tired

I reached out my hand for you to grab
you just push it away with a burning fury
I rip my heart in half to share with you
your anger has me so worried

You shout that you're not angry with a shaken
broken tone
your face as red as can be
You look through me with stale eyes telling me
your fine
you don't realize all that I see

Maybe one day you'll finally see
that your anger is so devastating
I fear by then it will be to late
I've grown so tired from all of this waiting

Don't Lose Yourself

He fought with me because that reflection in his
mirror would not fight back
Somehow projecting his feelings onto me made
him proud
Gaslighting his way into my head
brought out the worst in me
I became the reflection he hated
My image
a liar
My emotions
mixed
My molding
his twin
Looking into my mirror
eyes of worry looking back
a simple whisper
"You're losing yourself!"

Losing Myself

I've lost myself

Lost in the darkness called your love
My heart bleeds out
I've been convinced that this is true love

Throw your corruption at me
as you continue to cheat
I blindly agree
This must be what it's like
feeling incomplete

Pretending

Pretending I've moved on has become second
nature

Maybe if I keep telling myself I have
I finally will

Never Forget

I fell in love with the man that was hidden
inside
but he hid him very well
Hiding behind a hectic mind
and a strong need to rebel
In his tornado of love
he ripped apart my heart
Putting his needs well above
was only just the start
In the blink of an eye
We became estranged
The years went by
nothing had changed
That love I once felt
for the man that he hid
Would stay within me
forever dimmed

My Heart

I dive into my chest to see what is there
I yank it right out with such zest
with such flare
This blood pumping thing
lay right in my hands
It's grown heavy with a sorrow
I can't understand
By taking it out
maybe this will all end
Without it
I can never ascend
Looking at it shows
it only pumps blood and keeps me alive
Even though it's so full of feelings
of truths I cant archive
The feelings it holds
so heavy and numb
So much emotion
I can't overcome
So I take this misshapen object
and shove it back in
So in rushes those feelings
through the blood of my sins

Scribbles 1

to want love
is not the same
as wanting
to be loved

Destroying Me

He told me he loved me
then
spent everyday slowly
destroying me
What a vicious act

Unstable

I tried building on unstable ground
It's no wonder the walls came crashing down
around me

Becoming The Love He Gives

day after day he drills into my head
I'm Nothing
No one
over and over I play back everything he said
the nothingness grows
I'm No one
ripping away my sanity
slapping me full of guilt
filling me with insanity
desperation is now how I'm built
I hunger for his hate
he's created a perfect dependent
my self hate can now relate
I'll surely never cause disappointment

Cruel

This pain
I can't take it
I throw myself to the floor
He just laughs at me
calls me a fool
I break a little bit more

His cruelness
it's sickening
he steps over my vulnerable body
I'm breaking
so quickly
He makes this into his favorite hobby

Unheard

The tension here is so sharp
dripping with toxicity
The cold pain within my heart
sends shards of ice right through me

Those uncaring eyes just leering
his cold shoulder leaves me breathless
All his tainted words I'm still hearing
they are daunting and senseless

When the last tear falls
I'll await those meaningless words
Like it never mattered at all
I'll continue feeling unheard

Scribbles 2

Day after day
you continue to weaken me
and I allow it to happen

The Opposite of Love

Tell me how much you hate me
and that you wish you never met me
Then as I head for the door
beg me not to go?!

Leaving Broken

"*I hate you!*"
I said
as I walked out the door

Why Don't You Just Leave?

The #1 question!
I did
Several times
That wasn't even the hardest part..
Laying in bed at night with my trained mind
reeling,
"How can I do this on my own?"
"I need him to tell me what to do!"
"I need him to tell me what to think!"
"I'm so worthless, I don't know why I'm even
alive!"
"He was right, I can't do this!"
The thoughts he poured into my mind with his
mixing cup from Hell
took over leaving me feeling
Alone
Vulnerable
Not good enough
Until I finally gave in and went back
and that's when the
repetitiveness began

No Regrets

I will never regret
the love
I have foolishly given out

There was a time
when I too
sat in darkness
in need of love

Taking Hits

Go ahead
Tell me how awful I am
like I don't already feel it!
Gather all your pain and stab me in the heart!
I can take it
I will cry
But I can take it!

His Bitterness

He breathes stale words and conflict
No dreams or goals in sight
Anger
he is an addict
He lives
only to fight

Sorriness surrounds him
For his life is such a waste
He's allowed his light to go dim
Bitterness
is all he tastes

You Broke Me

I saw how much pain you were in
and
I simply walked away without a care

Helping Him

That moment I saw him sitting there in his own
agony
was the moment
I mistook
Love
with my strong desire
to help others

His View

This fury burns within
he treats me like a mistake
His very existence wears me thin
I'll throw words he just can not take
Treat me like the fool I am
my innocence has never existed
Your painful ways come flooding in
your view is so sick
so twisted

Coming To Life

The truth drips from my tongue
sending shards of your brokenness to you
You stand there looking stunned
at the truth only we both knew
You want to keep your secrets
of the way that you used me
I'll no longer keep them
let everyone fucking see
You can't beat me down anymore
I'm standing my ground
I will no longer ignore it
This goddess won't be bound!

Calling You Out

Suffering in silence
for too many years
no longer will I hide
my hopes
or my fears

I'll scream them all out
from the top of my lungs
releasing this pain from deep within my shouts
until clean blood drips from my tongue

These screams will reach you
no matter where you hide
you see
I'm no longer your well kept fool
I'm calling out your so called 'pride'

You've beat me while I'm up
you beat me when I'm down
Now you can drink
the poison from your own cup
You'll no longer see me frown

My words now flow like beautiful hot lava
canceling out the hate that you spew
No time left for your never ending drama
one day you'll grow tired of it to

To Alcohol's Lover

Looking through blurred eyes
stumbling across the floor
more drunk then he realized
she just can't compete anymore

He picks up another drink
hoping it numbs the pain
he hasn't found the link
for the reason he's insane

She asked him to choose
as it's been far to long
she'll be the one to lose
as he paints her as the one who's wrong

The lie's he let fill his head
they cripple him so
this lifestyle he cannot shed
it follows wherever he goes

Love Blind

Letting him in my home
was the biggest mistake I've made
I never felt his cold
until I began to ache
He sucked the life from me
put a doubt within my mind
How could I not see
I must have been love blind
Now anger fills the air
negativity
despair
How eagerly he shares
it all seems so unfair
That look in his eyes
he had hidden in the beginning
He must think he is so sly
like there's something he is winning
In truth he has won
I am utterly defeated
forgetting where I come from
My re-membering is needed

What I Deserve

When I was treated good
I believed
"I don't deserve this."
So I quickly ran into the arms of hate and anger

It only took years and years
to realize
I deserve what I allow

The Home to Blame

I blame **Love**
"It's all your fault!"
no such thing as truelove
one giant assault

Then I opened my eyes
and now can see
Love is not filled with lies
my heart can soon be free

It was really him
with his lack of knowledge on how to treat me
The way he loved so grim
his ability must have been lost at sea

No longer will I let this hold me back
my fear of **Love**
I've now fixed up all the cracks
on the search of all I've been deprived of

No Love

Maybe I only Love those who will hurt me
Maybe if I loved myself I wouldn't do this

No Fleeing Fates Hate

You beat me down with your words
now I know my worth
Leaving me impaired
I wonder what else will unearth

Cold feelings of hate
as if I couldn't see
I now accept my fate
these feelings I'll never flee

When Love Comes From the Fist

Distaste seeps from his pores
anger drips from his tongue
Visions of secret wars
come out when he is drunk
Slash me with your fury
kick me when I'm down
The beginning now is blurry
when hate is all that's around
I'll stay no longer
he has seen to this
He's grown such a hunger
to showing his Love with his fists

I'm Tired

I'm tired of the thousand messages I send
All thought out and perfectly written
All filled with secret meanings and the directions
on how to fucking love me!

Invalidation

ripping me apart
inside
out
knee's covered with the dirt of realization
my head throbs
heart torn
dying from his lack of validation

His Dominance

Staring at this page
my mind's feeling blank
I guess for this
it's you I have to thank
All this sorrow
leaves me feeling numb
You make me feel like I'm just
unpaid income
My walls once strong
built so high
You broke them all down
torturing me with your lies
Now here I am
left with broken promises
Are you happy now
that you've discovered some dominance

Dripping in Anger

His darkness cuts like a knife
slitting my heart from the inside out
I can't look him in the eyes
the blackness shows me what I've gone without
His mouth drips with anger
waiting to surround my throat
waiting for me to slip
keeping me on this tightrope
I fear I cannot survive
this feeling of great loss
Feeling like this is not
worth the beginning cause

Intention

I told you all my secrets and handed you the keys to my palace - Not realizing you just wanted the fire power to overtake my Home.

Deep Sadness

How did it feel to sit and watch me break?
Did you feel anything at all?
While I was feeling every bit of pain a human
could feel
I saw the look in your eye's
That look of nothing
I thought my heart was broken and sad before
now I've seen what true sadness is

Hand Me My Heart

He ripped my heart from my chest
put a crack in my soul
Our love once so intense
now our hearts have grown so cold
His hand I once held
now I shiver from the touch
His distance for me grows
at times I miss our love so much
Just package up my heart
leave it here for me
I'll put it back together
leaving behind these broken memories

Fire in the Stars

your forever came with an expiration date
my reaction was something to desire
if in the stars it's written my fate
that glistening light must be on fire

Forbidden Love

It was something he said that sent her spiraling
the ugly truth dripping from his lips
Only she could see the irony
how the Devil sold to her his partnership

Just one wish is how it started
that dark night with the stars so blindingly
bright
In search of a love so off the chart
if she only knew what she would ignite

His light came in like a volcano erupting
she would only see beautiful stars
She couldn't see all of the pain and corruption
she would only allow herself to see so far

Her blindness continued until she could no longer
breathe
she begged herself for forgiveness
The Devil will never allow her to leave
for she's the one who asked for a love so
forbidden

Enough

Getting used to the silence is hard
not having you as my person
You're right here yet so very far
this all just is not working

This quiet is just eating me alive
it has me all choked up
I'm so tired from all of these painful cries
when will enough be enough

The silence echoes right through me
leaving bitterness behind
If only you cared to see
but you'll sit there staring blind

I just can't take this anymore
so I'll start to open back up
Dropping my feelings onto the floor
like a volcano I begin to erupt

Cold To The Touch

Your hands are like ice
I get frostbite from a simple touch

Death Before I Die

His words wrap around my throat
strangling me unconscious
That look of fury sends slits to my already
scarred wrists
With every step I try being cautious
pounding the ground with hate filled fists
How can this man be so cruel
Why does he yearn to hurt me
Treating me like I'm nothing but a fool
there won't be much left to bury

The Battle to Loneliness

And so it begins
when you say that you care
I'll begin to let you in
you'll pull away with such flare
My heart always aches
I feel so trapped and alone
I'll do whatever it takes
to let it not be shown
So I sit here in wait
for you to hurt me again
You are surly never late
for this is a battle you always win

1 a.m. Thoughts

I never felt more alone in my life
than when I was sitting right next to you
Your cold shoulder is like an ice storm
Your anger is something meant for wars

Prolonging Fear

You see me through your hateful eyes
listen with tainted ears
The very thought of me shakes you to the core
you have me living my life in fear

A simple text says that you love me
aloud you tell me I'm a mistake
Alone at night I go to bed
I feel like I'm about to break

Your cold words linger in me all day
that hatred in your voice
You're here torturing me
as if I don't have a choice

I'm aware I haven't left
I've stayed here far to long
I need to break free from your chains
stop letting this fear be prolonged

Heartbreak

You've taken this heart
I've fully given to you
You loved it at first
this we both knew
Once you saw me
for who I really am
I guess I flunked
your final exam
The mistreatment started
and I felt like a fool
Showing my love
was quickly overruled
Spending your time
laying with them
While I was alone
feeling condemned
I gave my all
to a man so selfish
But I thought I loved you so much
I just couldn't help it
Saying goodbye to you
became so easy
Too many heartbreaks
have cut me deeply

Silent Heartbreak

This silence makes me uncomfortable.
The fact that after all this time, there's just
nothing left to say!

Self-Sabotage

I can't express just how hard it is to watch someone drown. Especially when the water's been dried up for years.

Sunday

Sunday afternoons
His abrupt personality
Mixing with the warmth
of his love
The sound of the little's laughter
A simple shared look
Time stood still

These were the moments
I held onto

Resist

he set me up for failure
his smug idea of love
pulling me in with his strong lure
believing I was loved
his sharp tone left me breathless
a sharp pain within my heart
feeling so helpless
falling apart
dark words to my ears
anger fills his fists
he'll eagerly share
no matter how much
I resist

Giving into the Cold

I gave my heart
to a day so cold
I gave my mind
just to watch everything fold
I felt my soul
fight to stay away
but here my body stayed

The words I gave
just weren't enough
My heart left
wanting to give up
These hands
held on so tight
Over and over
I gave into the fight

Wasted Life

He's dripping in lies
giving her life meaning
Listening to her cry
gives him that rewarding feeling
Sprinkling on the fear
gives her a better taste
Her name
he has smeared
Her life
such a waste

Moving on from my Fixing Habits

I wanted to fix it for you
the disappointment of your life
I became the fixer
more your helper than a wife
You took from me all you could
leaving me depleted
Time after time
you've left me utterly defeated
Excuses I would make
"he's just so sad and helpless"
I just could not see
my enabling was reckless
Going through this day after day
has exhausted my heart, soul, and mind
I need to move on with my life
leaving your victimization behind

This Man's Disguise

His deep dark eyes are so full of fury
his words as sharp as knives
Why is he always looking for a fight?
Does he care not, for his life?
Why he's here
he'll never know
He stays to himself
he sits alone
Does he wish to atone?
Does he wish to be alone?
His soul how it aches
sitting in silence
He wishes for a better place
away from his own violence
Maybe one day he will open his eyes
open them wide
let out his inner cries
Until then
he shall sit as he is
He shall wonder
he shall fight
Fight those battles deep inside
Such a sad soul
with wandering eyes
While I saw his potential
he hid behind a disguise

Remembering My Power

Nine long years he haunted me
the way I talked
walked
sat
and breathed
Forced his way into my head
he forced his way into my bed
Made me feel
I was worthless and dumb
Now my feelings so scared
my feelings so numb
I've pushed his voice
out of my mind
I kicked him out
this is now my time
Here he is
with words so cruel
Trying to make me feel
like I'm nothing but a damn fool
I am stronger then
he will ever be
His words are all he's got
The real power is in me

Manipulative Lust

When I open up to you
showing my whole heart
you throw your narcissism in my face
I was never able to differentiate
Love
for your need to have something over me

Questions

Do you ever look at me and actually see me?
All that I'm feeling?
All that I do?
All that I am?

Would it even matter?

In Sickness and in Health

I never feel good
You mistake that for not caring

Nightmares

I thought I pushed you out of my mind
but these things I'm seeing behind closed eyes
They shake me to my inner core
freaking out, I fall to the floor
I thought I finally escaped your clutch
but here you are bringing me down and such
How do I wash you from my mind
and wake up leaving you far behind

Lost

It's easy to get lost

In his eyes
filled with lies
In his heart
broken from the start
By his hand
taking me to bitter land

It's easy to get lost

More Questions

How many have you used?

                How many know my pain?

Am I the only one you abuse?

                What do you have to gain?

Invisible Ropes

The invisible ropes wrapped around my already
bruised wrists
must had been laced with barbwire
He'd come home and give my reluctant mouth a
kiss
his ego would grow a bit wider
He knew I would sit home like a good little girl
as he trapsed all over town
I must have thrown him for a whirl
the day I dropped those ropes to the ground
Too many years I sat right there
awaiting his approval
I was sick of watching as everyone stared
why did life with him have to be so brutal

Crumpled Lotus

When my thighs shook did that turn you on
did you think it was alright
Did you care to think that you might be wrong
as I shook with all my might

When I blacked out did you even notice
the darkness in my eyes
Or were you so deep in my lotus
that you didn't hear my cries

How quickly you were done and walking away
as I lay there on the floor
Standing there you had nothing to say
while my innocence was no more

Cancer of the Heart

terminate this cancer
the silent deadly pain
it comes out of nowhere
driving you insane
it lives deep inside
demanding so much attention
with nowhere to hide
it creates such terrible tension
this cancer has a name
a face
a feeling
trying to control
my space
my reason

Worthless Confusion

I await his return so that I may release these
inner pains
the thoughts that have taken over my mind
spinning my stomach in knots
The strength I have given to waiting
makes me proud
He walks in
I wait just a bit longer to not overwhelm him
His well being
more important to me
Strategically placing my words perfect for no
confusion
I think this is going to be good
as I begin to talk
I make sure to not make him angry
He is anyway
I thought if I worked my hardest he would
engage
Only
he yells
telling me all of my flaws
of the things I've done and continue doing wrong
of the reasons he hates me
All of my work went unnoticed
Suddenly I begin to feel
     Worthless

Loud Silence

We began to drift apart
You sat in silence while I screamed for you to
hear me
When it was time for you to listen
I stopped screaming
I sat in silence as you were screaming for me to
hear you
When I began to listen
you stopped screaming
sitting in silence
And this is how we would go on
until we were both
deaf
from each other's
high pitched
lonely pain

Oh how nice it is to be happy and calm.

—Until 4 p.m. when he gets home

A Never Ending Fight

He called me crazy
while showing his
I fought for our family
while he fought with himself

Unhappily Ever After

We got married so that we both had someone to
be unhappy with forever
I started to see how I didn't need this gut
wrenching unhappiness to survive
I began to find myself and the unhappiness
began to fade
That's when your panic began
Unhappiness consumed with anger
anger taking over
You either sit in silence
or tear me down
breaking my soul with your hateful words
Your hate for me grows to strong
with fire building up in your fists
I won't let you snuff out my light
You could care less for my protest
Unable to conform me
you bring forth more darkness
with a quick throw of your fist
incarceration is now my future
Bringing back unhappiness
so that we may live
unhappily ever after

Fuck His Words

When I see myself through your eyes
I feel so empty
so numb
Everything I hear
filled with lies
I just wait
for the bitter end to come

Why hurt a soul so deep
Are these tears not enough
As I sit here and weep
I realize I need to wake up

Breaking me down like this
only shows your hatred for yourself
This will not end in bliss
So fuck your words
I'm going to go find myself

End It

I hope you never push your hatred onto others as
you've done to me
those nightmarish feelings that you harbor
When darkness is the only thing you can see
please don't seek for a partner
Let it be with you
Let it end right here
the negative truth
an ending of fear

Another Beautiful Sunday

Sitting here all alone
doesn't bother me anymore
Knowing your in the other room
still leaves me feeling a little torn
My emotions mixed with yours
are to strong for me to bare
You sit there feeling fine
while I'm sitting in despair
I try to talk to you with reason
you push me right away
Your anger tells me all
it leaves nothing left to say
So I'll sit here all alone
lying to myself
Pretending I'm not bothered
all while living my life in hell

Challenged Lies

I challenged him
when I questioned him

Lies dislike
questions asked

Atone or Farewell

The voice of reason skipped over you
you have no care in all you do
Protect yourself and no one else
even when your closest relationships fell
This selfish behavior has left you alone
It's never too late if you wish to atone
You have to make the choice yourself
to take responsibility or to say farewell

Looking for that Strength

To hate you
Has been easy

To love you after all
you've done
takes a strength I do not yet know

Confused Words

You tell me you want to be better
You tell me you want to love me the way I
should be loved
You tell me I'm the biggest mistake of your life
You tell me you want a divorce

Overrated

When you told me I was worthless
I believed you wholeheartedly
Your words left me breathless
leaving darkness all over me
If this is how you love
I'd rather be hated
Within I'll find my own love
waiting for prince charming is overrated

Tornado

I was not strong enough
when his tornado came through
He took my everything
changed everything I knew

Selfish Ways

It was his selfishness
that overpowered his whole
Leaving me open and vulnerable
feeling out of control

Does he see what he's doing
does he even care
His game I am losing
it feels so unfair

Toxic Love

We were done
I had walked away
But you came back changed
or so I thought
A message from her
with a photo attached
left me feeling vulnerable
and under attack
My hope was so high
my love open and honest
Now on the floor I cry
broken in need of solace
How do I let you
play with my emotions so
I run back when you say the right words
This love is so toxic
I have to let it go
You will never change
for this I am sure

His Words

It was the way that he spoke
that got me hooked
I hung to every word
Something in me woke
something in me shook
all the darkness blurred

His words began to break
I was left defeated
Being drawn to him
a mistake
One I never wanted repeated

Was I His Drug?

Was I his drug?
maybe that's why he loved me
Looking deep into my eyes
with a hunger so fierce

Was I his drug?
So easily he walked away
when he yearned for more

Was I his drug?
Only not strong enough
not dangerous enough

If only he could drop
this habit
the way he
has dropped me

Unwanted Life

He took my youth with absolutely no care
feeling good about his accomplishment
He loved the attention when everyone stared
thinking they were giving him a compliment
I felt awful just wanting to go home
to a place that did not exist
The fear on my face overshown
this life was not what I wished
But here I was with beautiful life inside me
growing day by day
How quickly excitement was all I could see
this was a price I would gladly pay

Codependent

Today feels to Happy
I ache for your darkness to snuff out the light
Clearly my codependency is in full power

Harsh Love

I repeated the words he said to me
over and over in my head
Still they make no sense to me
I just cant comprehend

How do you say such harsh words
to someone you claim to love?
I find it absolutely absurd
This cannot be truelove

Deep Truth

These unclean words that are not true
Straight from my mouth straight to you
Like dirty knives filled with secrets
I let it all out I just cannot keep it
After all is said my mind feels empty
All those lies spread the truth can't be seen
I'm sickened by my manic ways and still feel so
confused
Why have you chosen to stay as if you have
something to lose
My love for you is so very strong
But the words that I use always seem wrong
When I'm scared I feel utterly alone
I know you're here but my fears are already set
in stone
All these years of walking out
being left behind and sitting in doubt
In fear of trust
of love
of truth
I fear that I have become my abuse

All the Heartbreaks Make Me, Me!

Where did your Heartbreak start?
When my inner child began to hurt
A mans hand up my skirt
Another cheating mystery
Living this life of misery

Scribbles 3

How is it that he hurt me
and I
comforted him

Alone and Unloved

I sit here with no one to talk to
while he sleeps his hard day away
He has no clue what I've been through
all this pain I go through everyday

I know he's growing frustrated
he's tired of my cries and my pain
If only he knew how much I hate it
how much I actually hold back and restrain

I question my reason on the daily
I just don't get my point
feeling like I'm going crazy
I hate that I constantly disappoint

I'm not the woman that he fell for
our love has changed so much
My devastated heart feels so torn
overwhelmed by this feeling of being unloved

An Enemy of Love

You transfer your words through me
like a dagger to it's enemy
the pain radiates over my entire heart and soul

I decide to send your pain back
so you're able to see
how much this all takes such a toll

Living in this chaos
has filled me with hate
my tongue has become my own enemy

Would starting over
give me a clean slate
I need space
to sort out this insanity

Thoughts

He has sucked the life out of me. What I once enjoyed now feels like a burden. Happiness that I once felt is so far from me. I don't remember its feels, its taste, its textures. His words cut through me in competition with this blade I hold dripping in the remains of my life force. Does he even care? What about how much I care? But how do I even know, when who I am has been pushed down to the deepest parts of the ocean. To the place no human can get to. Undiscovered, Lost. I'll sit with this pain as the bleeding tears drip, leaving all the hurt puddled upon my bed. Alone has been the safest and most dangerous place I can be. Away from the hurt but locked in my mind.

When She Bottles Her Feelings

She sits deep in her head
deafened by her heart
No longer can she play pretend
picking her love apart
She chokes back the tears
not agreeing with herself
Living in this fear
putting her feelings on the shelf
Safe away from feeling
now that they're bottled away
She'll be on her way to healing
the things she could never not say

A Frozen Heart

Years of ice cold feelings
leave a frost over my heart
The cold cripples me
with such an ache
My mind confuses
where this story actually starts
So many smiles
I've had to fake
Pushing forward
through blizzardous storms
My body
yearns to give up
This ache comes
in many forms
The snow begins to pile up
As the frost bite starts to settle in
tears of ice stay upon my face
This wintery day is one
that I will remember as a sin
This cold
I've now learned to embrace

Scribbles 4

I'm washing these walls of guilt with self hatred
and consuming all of your tortured words

Fear

Why can't I get up off my knees
stop begging for a love that doesn't exist
I guess I'm that scared of being lonely
even though I feel that with him anyway
My brain needs to be rewired
to stop being so afraid
Afraid of myself
of spending time with me
Afraid I won't work out
and that I won't like who I am

The Ending

We didn't leave on a strong note
just two people who weren't right for each other
going their separate ways

No

We murdered our relationship with
bad attitudes
finger pointing
terrible behaviors
and
plain ignorance

A Broken Girls Heart

My heart you have hurt
you ripped it out to digest
Covered in dirt
not ready to be addressed

As you lay there with those haunted eyes closed
I sit here questioning everything
Do you feel the strength of the opposed
because I'm feeling it with such agony

This pain goes so deep
I fear my soul has been affected
No matter how much I weep
the hurt was unexpected

The Beauty in Pain

I look at him and see such darkness
that shining light is now gone
My heavy heart worthless
no longer do I feel that loving song
The one that made me full
I could dance without a beat
It was so full of soul
one could get burned from all the heat
No longer do I see it
I now see the beauty with blurred eyes
I cannot stand the quiet
or all of these unheard painful cries
The dark has always scared me
the changes of a soul
I wish I could have foreseen
the pain and the beauty of letting go

Entrapping Possession

Handing me a ring does not mean you have me
wrapped around your weak-ass finger!
That chunk of metal can come off quicker than it
went on!

The Fire in Blurred Eyes

The beauty of this aching day
was lost in my fiery mind
The pain was strategically placed
throughout my entire mind's eye
The chaos that erupted
from such a tiny sliver of hate
Will never be completely lost
I've bolted it behind my minds locked gate

You take what I said and hold it so tight
that it's bleeding from your chest
These words so carelessly thrown around
I think there's nothing that I missed
To take them back now
would be a total lapse in judgment
as I meant every word
So here I'll sit in my dungeon like Hell
looking through eyes that are now only blurred

Going Through the Emotions

Thank you for the endless tears
my never ending fear
the stillness of my heart
the love that grew tart
my endless worry
this mind filled with fury
finding who I am
not letting you win
drinking up those tears
pushing through these fears
refilling my heart
that you ripped apart
fuck all these worries
I'm no longer feeling any fury

Love Lost

I look between these empty walls
Nothing is the same
The couch on which we sat together
Gone
The dinners we made
turned into takeout boxes for one
The love that was made on the floor of our new
place
now a distant memory
Overtaken by loneliness
Tears build
I sit here in full feeling
letting it wash over me
Until I feel the distance
no more
bring life to this ending

The Scent of Loneliness

It's that scent of bitterness
the smell of stale air
It's cold and darkness
nothing else seems to compare

It's echoing silence
brings a numbness to your ears
The body that lays next to you
just doesn't seem to be there
The space between
holds all of your fears
These fears you both
don't necessarily share

The touch feels of ice
you yearn to get warm
Your soul so full of life
but these feelings so warn

You tell yourself
it'll all be fine
As you sit
with a sadness so deep

This feeling has taken
so much of your time
Alone you sit
and weep

It's Just a Little Lie

Life isn't always what it seems
A man's disguise
A woman's broken heart
The telling of lies
People falling apart

The Cruelness of Opinions

Why are you so fucking cruel?
Your opinions are not my reality!

Out Of Touch

You have left me sitting in my silence
my agony too much to bare
This mind creates many different ways
all ending with the fact that you might care
My soul is searching for you
but you are nowhere to be seen
My heart races so fast
your still not there for me to lean
My soul is aching so bad
I'm feeling so very lost
I just want my best friend
Why are we so out of touch?

Starting Anew

Your dark words
split my soul in half
I let out
a crying laugh
Your hate so alive
it leaves me broken
This anger's
so outspoken
I won't let you take
from me anymore
I stomp my foot
to the cold and wet floor
I release your pain
back onto you
From here on out
I will start anew

Not Your Mother

He needed so much from me
If only he would realize that we were connected
just never by an umbilical cord

Scribbles 5

He tells me that I'm crazy
as if he wasn't the one who drove me there
Maybe being cruel to me
will cover up his affairs

Scribbles 6

You told me you loved stories
so I shared with you mine
I let the words pour from my mouth
tears drip from my eyes
You said you could handle it
but you were making your plan to run
the entire time

The Sting is Coming

If you don't acknowledge what I'm saying then we're not having this conversation. Your fucking logic sucks! By not acknowledging it means the power behind it is only growing stronger. The conversation Will be had and that good-bye that's coming? Damn, is that going to sting!

His Darkness

He said he didn't deserve me
but I sat with him in his darkness anyway
If only I knew he planned to have
his darkness swallow us both

The First Heartbreak

I should have known by the look in his eye
that he was trouble
The kind of trouble a girl on the run didn't need
His love started so subtle
I never realized until the moment I felt free
Free from running
Free from exhaustion
Oh how stunning he was
making me leave behind any and all caution
Then the earthquake of betrayal
left me broken
I began to spiral
leaving so much unspoken

Once Upon A Time

Once upon a time
  there was a girl
  She met her prince
  the one she longed for
  How quickly she no longer
  believed in fairytales

Scribbles 7

In his eyes
I see where I used to be
In his eyes
I see all of my old pain

Be Careful For What You Ask

I begged for love to come into my life
I didn't realize I would get exactly what I asked
for
Next time I'm going to need to be more specific!

A Bit to Far

When you told me I was crazy
I thought maybe I was
When you told me I loved the pain
I woke up and realized my worth

Distance

Our distance grows more with each day
my heart continues to ache
I never know the right things to say
I don't know what it will take

How do I turn this around
get my heart right
I can't make a single sound
without you thinking I'm trying to fight

While your coldness is in the lurk
I try to justify
This will simply never work
your thoughts of me are objectified

Blurred Past

Her soul was in pain
she didn't have a way out
Now she's learned of what's to gain
without ever having to shout
It's been here all this time
just waiting for her
To love is not a crime
her past
now a blur

Trauma

He yells through clenched teeth
his cheeks turning red
It pulls out that fear in her
the past plays in her head
For a moment everything turns black
and she replays that childhood pain
The next moment she'll never get back
that next moment she goes insane
He's brought out her inner demons
they've laid dormant far to long
They come out screaming
their voice loud and strong
He knows just what he's doing
his plan to pull this out
To her
he is not fooling
but she still gives into the shout
How angry she's become
at the happiness this brings him
How quickly she's undone
her light now fully dimmed

Awaken My Inner Bitch

With a sly smile I look at him
the worry builds in his eyes
I will swallow him whole
after he tells his agonizing lies
I am not that shy woman anymore
the one so naive
I shake him to the core
I'm not someone you deceive
I take his sick stories
rip them from his mouth
No need to worry
this will indeed be going south
Cry me a fucking river
of the blood you have forsaken
I embrace your deep shiver
giving breath to this life you have taken

My Ugliness

That ugly side of me came out again
the one that reacts without thinking
What he has started
I fight to win
my feelings begin sinking
Anger now consumes us both
as things fly through the air
I've now lost all of my control
cross me if you dare
How do I allow myself to get here
to this place I hate so much
When I'm filled with nothing but fear
I hold such a fierce grudge

Any Price

My demon
doesn't play well with others
My angel
will show you I'm just a lover
This pain I feel
goes way to deep
If I ask you to
will you show me your creep
This way it will save me
some much needed time
Find out now
that your just not mine
You don't want to scar me again
I'll show you that I always win
No matter what
the fucking price
I'll lay it all out
give it all my life

The Steps to Not Move On

Step 1: *Love*
Given out way too easily

Step 2: *Betrayal*
Easier than love

Step 3: *Forgiveness*
Why is it so hard?

Step 4: *Letting Go*
Error, go see Step 1

What do you Think of Love

*L*oss

*O*pposite

*V*ain

*E*nraged

I'm Sorry

You should have never watched me weep
never felt my pain
I fell in way to deep
bringing you with me again
My burdens were mine to bare
mine alone
That chaos got us nowhere
only to this broken home
I can't express just how much
my mistakes were never yours
I used you as my crutch
wanting for you to fight off all of my wars

Scribbles 8

My heart may be broken
but
it still beats!

Burning Cries

Another betrayal
time stands still
for a moment I forget who I am
No longer his lover
he gets his fill
my heart be damned
Why do I hold on so tight
when this is already over
Ending the day with another fight
another tiring cold shoulder
I pray for the day I can just walk away
the day I open my eyes
Leaving behind anything I'll ever need to say
leaving behind all these unheard burning cries

The Unforgettable

Tell me everything about you
and let me fall in love
I'll walk away feeling uneasy
all while falling short of
These large feelings I don't understand
that have taken me whole
They show up in mysterious ways
leaving me with no control
Anything good in my life
it comes and it goes
So I hold on very lightly
to anything that has arose
Say goodbye as I inevitably must
I'll think of you often
I'll live with these harbored feelings
you'll never be forgotten

Let it Fall

He has brought me to tears
I've finally had enough
For so many years
we've been living so rough
I'm sickened by his cruelness
the way he turns everything around
Always acting so foolish
he loves to put me down
He doesn't show any care
about anything at all
I've grown so uncomfortable and scarred
I have to let this fall

Good-Bye to the Past

Wishing to forever say goodbye
to these moments you present
It's obvious that I've
been a glutton for punishment
In every life I find you
the one who's wrong for me
If only I knew
right from the beginning
I could save myself the trouble
the lessons have been taught
Living these lives in struggle
my heart distraught
It's time to walk away
I no longer have it in me to stay
Saying goodbye to the past
Moves me forward
more than I could have guessed

Love / Hate

To save myself I had to walk away
Away from him and his love
Which looked a lot like
hate anyway

Rock Bottom

It's not an easy task at all
it takes you where you've never been
I had to take a few hard falls
I had to learn how to fend

To still love after so much loss
to believe with my whole heart
After paying the ultimate cost
after being completely torn apart

Here I am with my head held high
though tears are still streaming
Never thinking I'd be able to get by
that bottom is where I've found my meaning

My Worth

He found so many faults in me
while I overlooked his
It took walking away
to see my worth

Taking Back My Life

Under this rock I've been buried
safe from the actual truth
So much time spent worried
it's time to break through
Say goodbye to the shelter
that blocked me from seeing
You've been a soul collector
taking away my meaning
You feed off the fear
of my being all alone
Now I must take the wheel and steer
my life is finally my own

Thank You!

thank you for calling me all those names
thank you for putting me down
thank you for showing me hate
thank you for not sticking around

See
I realized

nothing you showed me was actually about me
it was all about you
your self hatred turned into my self hatred
but never again will I allow for you
to speak false words
show me your false actions
I have no time for your cold
you will no longer stop me from anything

Come On Home Dear

Come on home dear
I have dinner awaiting
your chair is ready
a cold beer on the stand
Come on home dear
I've paid all the bills
I've cleaned all the floors
everything is so tidy
Come on home dear
the children are quiet
after bath time and tantrums
I've made sure they're tucked into bed
Come on home dear
all clothes are ironed
the laundry all finished
I've set out your clothes for tomorrow
Come on home dear
I promise I wont show how tired I am
keeping a smile on my face
I'll wait on you hand and foot
Come on home dear
I'm so very sorry
that you lost your temper
I'll clean up your angry mess
Come on home dear
I didn't mean to make you angry
I promise I can do better
Come on home dear
please forgive me
I think I just need some rest

➜

Come on home dear
I know you've worked all day
and I have no job
I'll surely never complain again
Come on home dear
you are so right
I'm lazy and worthless
I wasn't appreciating all that you do
Come on home dear
how could I ever live without you
or stand on my own two feet
Come on home dear
before I realize
I am already doing this on my own
Your late dear
my bags are all packed
I know my worth
and I'm leaving you forever
So come home dear
you can mock yourself
clean up your mess
and enjoy your own anger
I'm so happy dear
living without you
no fear of compliance
you can no longer bring me down

Good-Bye

I asked you for help. Asking in a way other than words forming and spilling from my mouth like the acid rain they can be. It was a simple look of plea, a tear filled with pain, my mouth in the shape of a crescent moon spilling all of its magic onto the floor. No words needed. You just stood there looking through me like I was the invisible door to your fucking freedom. Now nothing could possibly stand in your way. But in your way of what? I was never standing in your way but by your side. One day you decided to stop while I was continuing to walk that path we both decided was for us. It then became my path and my path alone and you became bitter. I was to blame for your sudden lack of fucking knowledge on putting one foot in front of the other. I was now the obstacle you saw in your way to where you wanted to be. But who were we kidding? You had no damn clue what you wanted or where you wanted to be. So I'll ask for your help once more. But not in a simple look of plea or a tear filled with pain. My mouth will still be in the shape of a crescent moon spilling all of it's magic onto the floor, but, I'll realize quickly to flip that crescent moon around and collect back my magic. I realize words still won't be needed, but I'll use them anyway. 'Good-Bye!'

A huge shoutout to those who helped me see I can go that extra mile, I can get through hard times, I can ride the waves of this crazy life, and I can write the damn book! To my family, friends, and my writer's group - I thank you all!

Keep an eye out for my next book

The Scribbles of my Broken Life

Born with quite a unique Contradictory
Personality
Living in a small village in Upstate N.Y.
Raising two Awesome kids
Sipping tea through the chaos of life
Making Art with my words
And
Capturing Amazing Moments with my Camera
This is me...

Regina Ducey

www.ingramcontent.com/pod-product-compliance
Lightning Source LLC
Chambersburg PA
CBHW020250130626

46549CB00005B/2162